Without You

Without You

Without You

BY SARAH WEEKS · ILLUSTRATED BY SUZANNE DURANCEAU

SCHOLASTIC INC.
New York   Toronto   London   Auckland   Sydney
Mexico City   New Delhi   Hong Kong   Buenos Aires

When the female emperor penguin lays her egg, she passes it straight to her mate, who puts it in a pouch just above his feet. Unlike most birds, she doesn't stay to help protect her young; instead, she goes out to sea to feed, leaving the male alone with the egg for two months in the freezing Antarctic winter.

During that time the temperature drops far below zero, and the penguins live in total darkness. The males, each with an egg balanced carefully on his feet, live off only their own stored body fat.

Huddled together for
warmth, the vigilant emperors
constantly move and shift on the ice so that
each bird gets his share of protected time in the
warmer inner circle as well as on the chilly
perimeter, serving as a wind barrier for others. Soon
after the eggs hatch, the females return to the
colony. In the darkness the only way for the
birds to recognize each other is by their
voices, so they call to their mates as
loudly as they can. When the pairs
have reunited, the fathers gently
transfer the precious chicks to
the mothers' feet and go off
to sea to feed.

She'll come back to you
And me soon,
You'll see....

No sun shining down on us.
It's black as pitch all day.

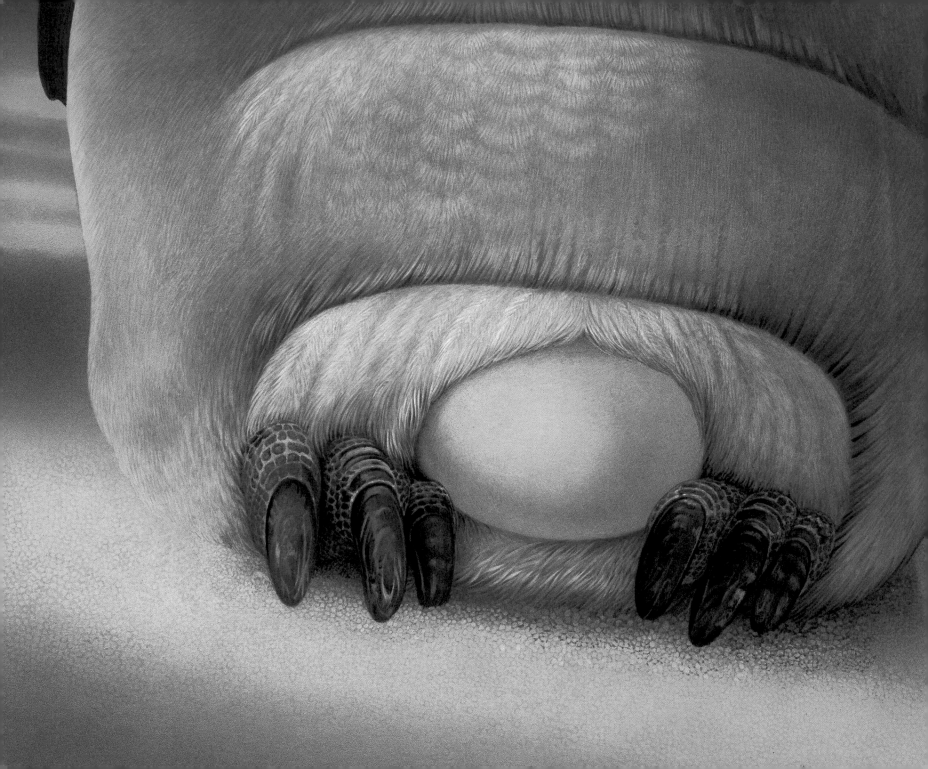

I feel a little funny inside.
My mamma's far away.

Nothin' but sea ice for miles around.
You close your eyes to the blinding sleet.
But here I am warm as toast,
Balancing on your feet.

Where would I be,
What would I do,
Who in the world would see me through...
Where would I be,
What would I do,
Without you?

We huddle together in the inner circle.

We serve our time on the outside too.

Brave the blizzards and the sad times,

While Mamma dives in the deep sea blue.

Nothin' but sea ice for miles around.
You duck your head when the cold wind blows.
But here I sit safe and sound,
Balancing on your toes.

Where would I be,
What would I do,
Who in the world would see me through…
Where would I be,
What would I do,
Without you?

I know that she's somewhere out there
Without us.

But I've got to believe
She's thinking about us.

She'll come back to you
And me soon,
You'll see....

No matter what,
You've got to stay awake now.
Don't let your eyes close.
When Mamma calls, you've got to answer for me.
Yours is the only voice she knows.

Where would I be,
What would I do,
Who in the world would see me through…
Where would I be,
What would I do…

Without you?

In loving memory of my
father, Robert Weeks.
–S.W.

This book is for you, Dad.
–S.D.

The illustrator would like to acknowledge Frans Lanting for the use
of some of his photographs as art references, courtesy of Minden Pictures.

ISBN-13: 978-0-545-04583-4
ISBN-10: 0-545-04583-5

Text copyright © 2003 by Sarah Weeks. Illustrations copyright © 2003 by Suzanne Duranceau.
All rights reserved. Published by Scholastic Inc., 557 Broadway, New York, NY 10012, by arrangement
with Laura Geringer Books, an imprint of HarperCollins Publishers. SCHOLASTIC and associated
logos are trademarks and/or registered trademarks of Scholastic Inc.

12 11 10 9 8 7 6 5 4 3 2 1   7 8 9 10 11/0

Printed in the U.S.A.   08
First Scholastic printing, September 2007

Typography by Alicia Mikles